ELIE WIESEL
Witness for Humanity

Life Portraits

ELIE WIESEL
Witness for Humanity

By Rachel Koestler-Grack

Gareth Stevens
Publishing

Please visit our web site at **www.garethstevens.com.**
For a free catalog describing Gareth Stevens Publishing's list of high-quality books,
call 1-800-542-2595 (USA) or 1-800-387-3178 (Canada).
Gareth Stevens Publishing's fax: 1-877-542-2596

Library of Congress Cataloging-in-Publication Data
Koestler-Grack, Rachel.
    Elie Wiesel: witness for humanity / by Rachel Koestler-Grack.
        p. cm. — (Life portraits)
    Includes bibliographical references and index.
    ISBN-10: 1-4339-0054-8   ISBN-13: 978-1-4339-0054-9 (lib. bdg.)
    1. Wiesel, Elie, 1928—Juvenile literature. 2. Jewish children in the
Holocaust—Biography. 3. Jews—Romania—Biography—Juvenile literature.
4. Holocaust, Jewish (1939-1945)—Romania—Biography—Juvenile literature.
I. Title.
DS135.R73W5445   2008
940.53'18092—dc22
    [B]   2008031630

This edition first published in 2009 by
Gareth Stevens Publishing
A Weekly Reader® Company
1 Reader's Digest Rd.
Pleasantville, NY 10570-7000 USA

Copyright © 2009 by Gareth Stevens, Inc.

Executive Managing Editor: Lisa M. Herrington
Creative Director: Lisa Donovan
Cover Designer: Keith Plechaty
Interior Designers: Yin Ling Wong and Keith Plechaty
Publisher: Keith Garton

Produced by Spooky Cheetah Press
www.spookycheetah.com
Editor: Stephanie Fitzgerald
Designer: Kimberly Shake
Cartographer: XNR Productions, Inc.
Proofreader: Jessica Cohn
Indexer: Madge Walls, All Sky Indexing

Printed in the United States of America

1 2 3 4 5 6 7 8 9 12 11 10 09 08

TABLE OF CONTENTS

Jewish people from all over Nazi-occupied Europe, including Elie and his family, were transported to concentration camps such as Auschwitz.

CHAPTER ONE

LOOK AT THE FIRE!

FIFTEEN-YEAR-OLD ELIEZER WIESEL STOOD WITH his father, mother, and three sisters pressed tightly against him. They jostled and swayed with the movement of the train, but no one fell down. The Wiesels were just six of the 80 people packed tight in the cattle car, shoulders overlapping like shingles on a roof. They could not lie down. There wasn't even room to sit unless they took turns.

The muggy air was suffocating and tasted of fear. With every gasp, the people on the train inhaled one another's breath. When they first stepped into the train car in late May of 1944, Hungarian police had given them some bread and a few pails of water. Now, two days later, the water was almost gone. The captives carefully rationed the bread. Elie's stomach twisted with hunger, but they had to save something for the next day. As bad as today was, tomorrow could be worse.

On the third day of the journey, the train screeched to a stop. The heavy door slid open to reveal a German officer. "From this moment on," he said, "you are under the authority of the German Army. There are 80 of you in the car. If anyone goes missing, you will all be shot like dogs." The door slammed shut and Elie heard the pounding of a hammer. They were being sealed in. Panic pounded inside the boy's empty stomach.

Eventually, Elie's exhaustion became more powerful than fear. He and his sisters huddled on the floor and fell asleep. Suddenly, a piercing cry startled Elie awake. A woman named Mrs. Schächter was screaming. "I see a fire!" she screeched. "I

The Transports

Jews from all over Nazi-occupied Europe traveled by railroad to concentration camps. As many as 100 people were crammed into each small cattle car. They had just pails of water, no bathroom, and no food. Barely any fresh air slid through the slim cracks in the walls. After traveling for several days and nights, deportees arrived at camps exhausted and confused. There, doctors determined their fate. Mothers with little children, the old, and the sick were sent to gas chambers. They were dead within hours of arrival. People over the age of 18 who could work moved on to a labor camp. At these camps, the prisoners were often worked to death.

see a fire!" Others in the car stretched their necks to see out the barred windows. There was nothing outside but black sky. Mrs. Schächter's 10-year-old son clung to his mother's skirt, crying, trying to calm her, but there was no soothing her. "Jews, listen to me," she shouted. "I see a fire! I see flames, huge flames!"

Elie knew Mrs. Schächter. She was a kind lady. Now she seemed to be possessed by some evil spirit. She just wouldn't stop screaming. Soon her outbursts

> "There are 80 of you in the car. If anyone goes missing, you will all be shot like dogs."
>
> – GERMAN ARMY OFFICER

became unbearable. A few young men forced Mrs. Schächter to sit down. Then they gagged her. Once again the night fell silent, except for the rhythmic rattling of the train and the muffled sobs of Mrs. Schächter's son.

Elie managed to doze off again when, suddenly, more screams jolted him awake. Mrs. Schächter had broken free from her bonds. "Look at the fire!" she shouted. "Look at the flames! Flames everywhere." Again, the men tied Mrs. Schächter up. This time, they rained punches on her, striking her repeatedly in the head. Her son, frozen with fear, stopped crying.

At last, Mrs. Schächter settled down and stared off into the distance. All the next day, she sat motionless and mute, her eyes empty and unfocused. It was as if she no longer knew or cared where she was. Near evening, though, she began ranting again.

Elie was almost relieved when they pulled into a station the next day. He just wanted to get away from the screams. "The heat, the thirst, the lack of air, were suffocating us," Elie recalled

Elie and his family traveled these railroad tracks into the entrance of Auschwitz. At this point, the prisoners had no idea what was about to happen to them.

years later. "Yet all that was nothing compared to her screams, which tore us apart." Someone near the window read the sign: AUSCHWITZ.

The officers told the people on the train that this was their final destination. They claimed the living conditions were good and families would stay together. Elie felt some of his anxiety start to melt away. Maybe there was nothing to fear. He and his family thanked God that the horrible journey was over, and that they were safe. Still sealed in the car, Elie and the others waited for the doors to open, but no one let them out. The afternoon slowly crept by. At about 11:00 at night, the train began to inch forward. Fifteen minutes later, it screeched to a halt again. They had arrived at a part of Auschwitz called Birkenau.

Suddenly, a terrible scream filled the night. "Jews, look!" Mrs. Schächter cried out. "Look at the fire! Look at the flames!" This time, when they looked out the window, Elie and the others

"Jews, look! Look at the fire! Look at the flames!"

– MRS. SCHÄCHTER

saw a chimney in the distance. It was spitting flames into the black sky. As the stench of burning flesh reached Elie's nose, the door flew open. Men jumped into the freight car and began

Auschwitz

Auschwitz was Nazi Germany's largest concentration and extermination camp. Located in southern Poland, near the city of Auschwitz, it actually consisted of three camps. Auschwitz I was the base camp and central office. This was the first stop at Auschwitz. Auschwitz II, or Birkenau, was an extermination camp. For prisoners there, the smell of burning flesh was a constant reminder of their fate. Auschwitz III, also known as Monowitz, was a forced labor camp. Buna, the subcamp where Elie and his father ended up, was part of Monowitz. It is estimated that by the end of the war between 1.1 million and 1.5 million people had been murdered at Auschwitz. Ninety percent of those killed were Jews. An additional 83,000 Poles and 19,000 Roma, or Gypsies, also died there.

swinging clubs at those inside. "Everybody out!" they yelled, as they struck the people in the car with their clubs. "Leave everything inside. Hurry up!"

Elie had no way of knowing, but he had arrived at the notorious Nazi death camp. He was one of at least 1.3 million people deported to Auschwitz during the Nazi reign of terror. Upon arrival, about 70 to 75 percent of the people on any given transport were sent to death without ever being registered. For that reason, the total number of people killed at the camp can only be estimated. What is known for sure is that of all the people sent to Auschwitz, Elie and about only 200,000 others survived. His grandmother, mother, father, and little sister were among the many dead.

> "I can only see myself as a witness. It is the witness in me that moves me to write, to teach, or to say things that are important to me."
>
> – ELIE WIESEL

At times, Elie almost lost his will to go on living. Somehow, though, he survived. For a long time, he wondered why he had lived when so many others died. As the years passed, the answer became clear. This ordinary boy from Sighet would go on to become a beacon of hope in the fight for human rights. Wherever people where persecuted or oppressed, wherever there was a victim who could not speak in his or her own defense, Elie lent his voice.

Today, Elie is a voice for humanity. He has written more than 40 books. He also joins the ranks of other concerned leaders and celebrities, such as George Clooney, who speak out for those

On September 14, 2006, Elie and actor George Clooney spoke out on behalf of the victims of genocide in Darfur, Sudan. Both men have worked to raise awareness and spark action by providing a voice for those suffering in the African region.

who are suffering around the world. He bears witness to those who survived the Holocaust as well as those who were not as fortunate. Elie also carries the message that such an atrocity should never happen again. "I can only see myself as a witness," he has said. "It is the witness in me that moves me to write, to teach, or to say things that are important to me." ❖

When Elie was a little boy, his hometown seemed safe from the growing threat of Hitler's Nazi regime. By the time Elie reached his teen years, however, the Nazis were moving ever closer to Sighet.

CHAPTER TWO

A FEW YEARS OF HAPPINESS

ELIEZER WIESEL WAS BORN TO SHLOMO AND SARS (Sarah) Wiesel on September 30, 1928, in the town of Sighet, in what is now Romania. At the time, Sighet was in the country of Transylvania, which later became part of Hungary. Elie had two older sisters, Bea and Hilda. When Elie was 7 years old, his little sister Tzipora was born. The entire family was madly in love with her. They pampered her, spoiled her, and showered her with all the love in their hearts.

Elie lived in a mostly Jewish neighborhood, where his father owned a small grocery store. Almost the entire town observed sacred days, such as Passover, Rosh Hashanah, and Yom Kippur. Elie felt a great sense of unity with his community.

Like other children in his neighborhood, Elie attended *heder,* a school for Jewish students. His first teacher was the Batizer Rebbe. He taught Elie the 22 letters of the Hebrew alphabet and introduced him to the Torah. The Torah is the Jewish Bible, known to non-Jews as the Old Testament. When Batizer Rebbe read the first word aloud—*Breshit,* or "in the beginning"— Elie felt like he had been transported to an enchanted universe. Reading the ancient texts of the Torah filled Elie with awe. There was something both fascinating and terrifying about the stories. For Jews, words are holy. When they pick up a sacred book, they kiss it. From a very young age, Elie read everything he could get his hands on. He always felt hungry for more knowledge.

Elie did not play outside much as a child. He spent his time in the schoolroom or synagogue. Most of the day, he buried his nose in books, although he did enjoy playing chess. Every Friday after school, Elie visited his Grandma Nissel, who lived alone

Wandering Teachers

Sometimes wandering teachers came through Sighet. With no homes, they would stay only for one night, and Elie would never see them again. The young boy loved to listen to their stories. As the teachers spoke of distant lands, Elie felt like one of their companions on a fantastic journey. During winter, the teachers would sleep in the synagogue. Elie would stay there very late at night to listen to their lessons. Because of these wanderers, Elie came to adore strangers. They bring stories, memories, and ideas from faraway places.

During Elie's childhood in the 1930s, Sighet was a typical Jewish town. Life revolved around family, the community, and observance of religious holidays.

after her husband (Elie's grandfather) died. "Eliezer, my boy, come, I'm waiting for you!" she would call from the window. When Elie sat down, Grandma Nissel placed a plate of fresh, warm buns in front of him and watched fondly as he recited his prayer. As he ate his treat, Elie would tell his grandma about everything he had learned that week.

Elie adored his father but never got a chance to spend much time with him. Shlomo was preoccupied with the little grocery store he owned. He also spent a great deal of time helping other Jewish people who were in need. Shlomo was well known throughout the community for his intelligence and kindness. People often came to him for advice. Rich or poor, friend or stranger, Shlomo welcomed anyone for any reason. As a child, Elie sometimes felt his father had time for everyone but him.

LIFE LESSONS

Shlomo taught Elie to care for other people. Even though the Wiesels were poor, they never hesitated to offer food to anyone who was hungry. One day a week, the family would set out a huge cauldron of bean soup in the yard for the beggars who roamed from village to village. "How can I tell which ones are really hungry?" Maria, the family servant, once asked Shlomo. "Don't try," he replied. "I'd rather feed someone whose pockets are full than send someone away on an empty stomach."

> **"I'd rather feed someone whose pockets are full than send someone away on an empty stomach."**
>
> – SHLOMO WIESEL

Shabbat was the only time Elie spent with his father. Shabbat began on Friday afternoon in Sighet. At the beginning of Shabbat, Elie would take a ritual bath—a special bath to purify himself. Then he would walk with his family to services at the synagogue. Sometimes, Shlomo would take Elie's hand along the way. With his small hand tucked inside his father's fist, Elie felt like they were bound to each other, and the rest of the world disappeared.

While Elie was growing up, Adolf Hitler was coming to power. Hitler was a vicious anti-Semite, and he used his power to make Jews suffer. In 1933, Hitler became chancellor of Germany. His supporters, the Nazis, began persecuting Jews immediately. Hitler's ultimate goal was to create a German "master race" by eliminating all people he considered subhuman. This included Jews, Gypsies, homosexuals, and the mentally and physically challenged. Then, in 1938, the Nazi regime took control of Austria. Hitler's power was spreading. Pogroms, or murderous riots, broke out against the Jews. When Germany invaded Poland in September 1939, World War II (1939–1945) began. In January 1942, the Nazis began the systematic deportation of Jews from

Breeding Anti-Semitism

Adolf Hitler and other members of the Nazi political party believed that they were superior to all other people. Hitler especially hated Jews. In speeches, he blamed all of Germany's problems on the Jews. After World War I (1914–1918), Germany was on the brink of ruin. It had lost all the territory it had gained in the war. Germany went from being the most powerful nation in Europe to having no power at all. The country was also entering an economic depression that would make its money basically worthless. Even though most Jewish people were hardworking, law-abiding citizens who had been loyal to Germany, Hitler wanted someone to blame for the country's troubles. Many people believed him and supported him.

Adolf Hitler came to power in Germany in 1933. He blamed the Jews for Germany's hard times and launched a plot to exterminate them.

all of Europe into six extermination camps in German-occupied Poland, including Auschwitz. This step was part of what Hitler called "The Final Solution," the Nazi plan of genocide to exterminate the Jewish people. (Genocide is the extermination of an entire race or group of people.) By the end of the war, as many as six million Jews died at the hands of the Nazis. This mass murder is known as the Holocaust. Every day, the Nazis moved closer to Hungary—and Sighet.

At the time, world events had little effect on Elie. He was too young to understand politics. He had heard murmurs about German victories in Europe and North Africa. It all seemed so distant and unreal, however, to the people of Sighet.

TROUBLE NEARBY

On the other hand, the situation closer to home terrified Elie. Anti-Semitism wasn't limited to Germany. People throughout Europe persecuted the Jews because of their religious beliefs. People would beat up Jews in the streets. Others painted graffiti on Jewish shops, telling the Jews to leave the country. Stories of pogroms reached Sighet from towns throughout Europe.

It was hard for the little boy to understand something like anti-Semitism. Elie asked his teachers why certain people hated the Jews so much. His teachers told him to read the sacred texts. Jewish history was flooded with suffering. Throughout the centuries, the Jews were in constant conflict with others. Ever since Abraham—the Old Testament patriarch—they would say, the Jewish people have been on one side and the rest of the world on the other. They reminded Elie to accept the persecution instead of becoming part of the violence. "Better to be among the victims than among the killers," one teacher said.

> "Better to be among the victims than among the killers."
>
> – ELIE'S TEACHER

Elie loved these stories. He read and reread the Torah and was especially interested in the prophets and martyrs—those who suffered and died for their faith. He sometimes wondered if he would have had the strength to endure persecution like the prophets of old. Never in his most terrifying nightmares could Elie have imagined that his own faith would soon be put to this type of test. ❖

Some transports never arrived at concentration camps. The Jews were ordered out of the cars, shot, and buried in mass graves. Often, Nazi soldiers forced the Jews to dig their own graves before they were killed.

CHAPTER THREE

ANGEL OF DEATH AT THE CITY GATES

I N 1941, WHEN HE WAS 13 YEARS OLD, ELIE MET
Moishe the Beadle. The frail man with a long, white beard
was a traveling teacher. He stopped in Sighet and decided
to stay. Elie and Moishe met almost every evening at the synagogue to interpret the Torah.

Then, near the end of 1942, all foreign Jews were expelled from
Sighet. Months passed without word of the deportees. Then one
day Elie saw Moishe sitting on a bench near the entrance of the
synagogue. The boy's happiness quickly turned to confusion as
Moishe told him what had happened to him. After the deportees
crossed into Polish territory, everyone was ordered off the train.
Waiting trucks transported them to a nearby forest. There, the
people were forced to dig huge trenches. They were digging their
own graves. One after another, the Gestapo shot the prisoners.
They even killed children and babies. Like the others, Moishe

was shot, but he had only been hit in the leg. The Gestapo left him for dead. After they were gone, Moishe escaped. He was the only one.

Moishe made his way back to Sighet to warn people about what he had seen. He went from one Jewish house to the next, telling his tale of horror, but no one listened. Such cruelty, such evil was just simply unimaginable for them. It seemed more reasonable to believe that Moishe had gone mad. Even Elie couldn't believe the things his teacher was saying. "I wanted to return to Sighet to describe to you my death so that you might ready yourselves while there is still time," Moishe explained to the boy. The joy that once filled his eyes had drained away. He no longer sang or spoke of God. "Life? I no longer care to live," he said. "I am alone. But I wanted to come back to warn you. Only no one is listening to me."

The Gestapo

The Gestapo was the secret Nazi police force. When the Nazis took over new territories, members of the Gestapo would round up Jews and send them to concentration camps or simply kill them. The Gestapo held the power of *Schutzhaft*, or "protective custody." This term was a flowery way of saying the officers could do whatever they wanted without fear of punishment. Jews had to do whatever the Gestapo ordered without question.

Elie knew that Jews were persecuted, but he did not know that they were being murdered. In his young mind, such cruelty did not seem possible. Although he loved his teacher, he did not believe his story.

On Sunday, March 19, 1944, Elie was studying at the synagogue when a man burst through the door. "Have you heard the news?" the man shouted frantically. "Don't you know what's going on? You sit here praying while the Angel of Death stands at the city gates!"

> **"You sit here praying while the Angel of Death stands at the city gates!"**
>
> – ELIE'S NEIGHBOR

The Germans had crossed the border. Hungary was occupied. No one in the congregation seemed too worried, though. Perhaps this messenger was just overreacting, they thought. Maybe he was a madman like Moishe. As the man ranted, waving his hands frantically, Moishe the Beadle stared silently ahead. He knew what was to come.

In April, German army vehicles rumbled into Sighet. SS soldiers, of the German *Schutzstaffel,* or "Protective Squadron," wandered the streets. For a child like Elie, it was hard to know what to think, how to feel. The officers seemed polite. Some even stayed in the homes of local Jews. Many people felt a bit relieved. "Where is their famous cruelty?" they asked.

Then, in late April, a series of decrees was issued. The Nazis arrested the leaders of the Jewish community and ordered all Jewish stores and offices to be closed. No Jew was allowed to go out, except in the later afternoon to buy food. Every Jew was to

The Protective Squadron

SS stands for the German word *Schutzstaffel*, which means "Protective Squadron." Adolf Hitler originally created the SS as his personal bodyguard unit. The SS soldiers were volunteers. Later, the SS became the core of the Nazi terror operation, which persecuted and tortured the Jews. The SS Death's Head Units ran the concentration camps.

wear a yellow star. Even though Elie knew that the star would bring ridicule from non-Jewish people, he wore it with pride. In fact, the star made him feel more intimately bound to other Jews. "No, I was not afraid of the yellow star," he later wrote. "But the posters that suddenly appeared on the walls were something else." These posters threatened that anyone who opposed the new order would be shot. "Shot?" Elie remembers thinking. "I didn't believe it, couldn't believe it, but my legs trembled."

THE GHETTO

In early May, the German officers created two ghettos in Sighet. These were enclosed portions of the city where all the Jews were forced to live. A large ghetto in the center of town stretched over four streets. A smaller one covered several alleyways on the outskirts of town. Elie's family lived on Serpent Street, in the large ghetto. The ghettos were cut off from the rest of the town by twisting barbed wire. The Jews had to stay inside the fences.

In a way, the ghettos did not seem like such a bad thing to Elie. His family was all together inside the ghetto, as were all the other Jewish people in town. The ghetto was like a tiny Jewish country. Their eyes no longer had to meet hateful stares. They could live without fear or anguish. Most people thought they would stay there in the ghetto until the end of the war. On the radio, they had heard that the Red Army—the Russian liberators—were fast approaching. They thought that one day very soon, the Russians would come and rescue them. "The ghetto was ruled by neither German nor Jew," Elie later said. "It was ruled by delusion [wild imagination]."

SS soldiers helped organize attacks on Jews across Europe. They were also responsible for the running of the Nazi death camps.

This Nazi propaganda poster features a picture of the Jewish star and reads, "Whoever wears this symbol is an enemy of our Volk [nation]." Posters such as this could be found all over German-occupied Europe.

Then, one night in May, a single word brought darkness to every heart: transports. Starting the next day, the ghetto would be emptied, street by street. The residents did not know where they were going. They were told only that each of them could bring a backpack of personal belongings, some food, and a few pieces of clothing—nothing else.

People in the ghetto stayed up all night preparing for the journey to an unknown destination. They dug holes in which to bury their family treasures. That night, Elie and his family became like gravediggers, burying pieces of their lives. Shlomo buried jewelry and important papers. Elie's little sister buried her toys. Crouched in the garden, Elie buried the only gift he had ever received—a gold watch that had been his grandfather's.

By 8:00 in the morning on May 16, the police stormed the streets shouting, "All Jews, outside! Hurry!" Anyone who moved too slowly—including old men, women, little children, and the disabled—were hurried along by the butt of an officer's rifle. "The time has come," they snarled. "You must leave all this."

DEPORTATION

Within two hours, everyone was outside. The people who were leaving on the first transports were told to line up. The police took roll call—once, twice, 20 times. The scorching sun beat down on the people's faces, and children cried for water. There was water close by—inside the nearby houses—but those in line were forbidden to move. Elie and his sisters were to leave on the last transport. They were still allowed to move about, so they filled water jugs and carried them to the people in line.

At 1:00 in the afternoon, the soldiers gave the signal for the first group to leave. One after another, they passed by Elie. Teachers, friends, people he had known his whole life disappeared around

In May 1944, Jews in Sighet faced deportation. They were forced to leave their homes and other belongings behind. Many never returned.

the corner, fading like ghosts into memory. After they were gone, Elie looked around. Here and there, little pieces of people's lives were strewn about: briefcases, bags, dishes, papers, and faded portraits. The deportees had planned to take it all along, but in the final moments before leaving, these material things suddenly seemed unimportant. "Open rooms everywhere. Gaping doors and windows looked out into the void," Elie later recalled. "It all belonged to everyone since it no longer belonged to anyone. It was there for the taking. An open tomb."

> **"Gaping doors and windows looked out into the void. It all belonged to everyone since it no longer belonged to anyone. It was there for the taking. An open tomb."**
>
> – ELIE WIESEL

Two days later, the scene was repeated. This time, Elie and his family would leave. "All Jews, outside!" Elie heard the soldiers shout. He and his family were ready. Elie went out first. He did not look at his parents' faces. He was too afraid he might burst into tears. The deportees stood in the street just like the others had, in the same sweltering heat. Only this time, there was no one to bring them water. Elie drank in the sight of his house from the middle of the street. He wondered if he would ever see it again.

Finally, they were ordered to march. Shlomo was crying. It was the first time Elie had ever seen his father cry. He felt as if his heart were breaking. Seven-year-old Tzipora carried a backpack that was far too heavy for her. The little girl clenched her teeth and uttered no complaint. Even at her young age, Tzipora under-

Jews were packed into cattle cars, and the doors were sealed closed. Very little light or air reached the people trapped inside these boxes.

stood that it was useless to complain. From time to time, the police would swing their clubs and shout, "Faster!" The journey had only just begun, and already Elie felt like he had no strength left. The Hungarian police ordered them to run, and so they ran. Already, Elie had begun to hate them, his first oppressors. When they finally arrived at their temporary destination—the small ghetto—they collapsed to the ground.

They were expelled a few days later at dawn. Elie and the others were marched to the railroad station, and crowded into cattle cars. A long and whining whistle blew as the wheels began to grind. The transport slowly pulled out of Sighet, forever separating Elie from the life he knew. ❖

People faced their first selection when they got off the train at Auschwitz. The elderly, children, anyone unfit for work, and many women were sent to their deaths. Others, including Elie, were moved to labor camps.

CHAPTER FOUR

Work Makes You Free

WHEN THE TRAIN ARRIVED AT AUSCHWITZ, SS officers kept their machine guns aimed at the people climbing out. One of them shouted, "Men to the left! Women to the right!" With those eight short, simple words, Elie's family was broken apart forever. He watched his mother, grandmother, and sisters disappear into the mass of prisoners. He had no way of knowing it was the last time he would ever see his grandmother, mother, or little Tzipora. It all happened so fast, there was little time to think about what was happening. There wasn't even time to say good-bye. "I didn't know that this was the moment in time and the place were I was leaving my mother and Tzipora forever," he later explained. Elie felt his father's hand press against his. They were alone. As his mother, grandmother, and sisters marched out of sight, Elie walked on with the men, holding tight to his father's hand.

As they walked, a gunshot rang out. Elie saw an old man behind him topple to the ground. Seconds later a nearby SS officer put his revolver back in its holster. Elie squeezed his father's hand in terror. Elie was not afraid of dying. He was afraid of being left alone. The SS officers ordered the men to form ranks, or lines, of five. Selection was about to begin. Only strong men would be chosen to live. All others—the young, old, and weak—would be sent to their deaths in the gas chambers.

Death Factories

Each camp in Auschwitz had its own crematorium and gas chambers. Women with small children, the elderly, and the weak were sent to the gas chambers immediately on arrival at Auschwitz. Elie's grandmother, mother, and little sister joined that line. Officers told the prisoners that they were going to be disinfected in a shower so that they would not panic. Nazi officers packed as many victims into the chamber as possible, and then sealed the door. A lethal gas was sprayed into the room, suffocating everyone inside. The pain and horror were unspeakable. Mothers and children died clinging to each other. A unit of prisoners called the *Sonderkommando* moved the dead bodies from the gas chambers to the crematorium. Flames shot from the chimney day and night, filling the entire camp with a sickening smell of burning flesh.

At the crematorium, ovens blazed day and night. Other prisoners were forced to perform the grisly task of cremating the dead.

A veteran inmate—someone who had been a prisoner for a while—leaned over to Elie. "Hey, kid, how old are you?" he asked. "Fifteen," Elie answered. "No," the man replied. "You are eighteen." Elie was puzzled. "But I'm not," argued Elie. "I'm fifteen." The man quickly grew angry. "Fool," he barked, "listen to what I say." This man understood the selection. He knew who would be allowed to live and who would be sent to the gas chambers. Turning to Shlomo, the man asked him the same question. Elie's father told the man he was fifty years old. "No," the man said, his voice growing even angrier. "Not fifty. You're forty. Do you hear? Eighteen and forty." After that, the man disappeared into the darkness.

In the distance, Elie could see flames clawing at the dark sky. He was looking at the crematorium. That is where bodies were thrown into the fire and burned to ashes. The smoke billowed from the chimney day and night, a constant reminder that death was never far away.

AMONG THE LIVING

Elie was stunned and petrified. He couldn't understand what was happening. Before he knew it, he found himself standing before an SS officer. "Your age?" he asked. "I'm eighteen," Elie said, his voice trembling. "Your profession?" asked the officer. Elie heard himself lie, "Farmer." This profession required strength, and strength would keep him alive. The officer pointed to the left. Shlomo also went left.

Elie was glad he and his father were together, but he wondered where their line led. Nearby, monstrous flames leapt out of a ditch. As Elie watched, a truck pulled up. The officers quickly began unloading its cargo into the fire. Elie strained to see what it was. He could hardly believe his eyes. The SS officers were feeding the blaze with the bodies of little children.

A little farther down the road, there was another fiery ditch—a larger one. Perhaps this pit was for adults, Elie thought. By this time, Shlomo was weeping, as were all the other men around him. They were reciting Kaddish—the Jewish prayer for the dead. Elie had never before heard this prayer said for the living.

Elie's forehead was covered with cold sweat. As he marched beside the barbed wire fences, his line moved closer and closer to the pit. He could feel the heat on his skin. For a moment, Elie considered suicide. Years later, he wrote about the thoughts that raced through his mind that night:

Twenty more steps. If I was going to kill myself, this was the time. Our column had only some fifteen steps to go. I bit my lips so that my father would not hear my teeth chattering. Ten more steps. Eight. Seven. … Only four more steps. Three. There it was, very close to us, the pit and its flames. I gathered all that remained of my strength in order to break rank and throw myself onto the barbed wire. Deep down, I was saying good-bye to my father.

Above the entrance to Auschwitz was a sign that read, "Work makes you free." Elie quickly realized that he and his father had little hope for freedom.

Just two steps from the ditch, the men were ordered to turn left, toward the barracks. That day, they would not die. "Do you remember Mrs. Schächter, in the train?" Shlomo asked his son. Of course Elie remembered the woman and her visions of fire. How could he forget?

Elie, his father, and the other men were stripped, shaved, disinfected, and forced to shower. Then they were dressed in thin cotton prison uniforms. After that they were sent to their barracks. These were brick buildings filled with two- and three-tier wooden slab bunk beds. Suddenly, an SS officer appeared in front of them. He told them in cold, hard words that they were in a concentration camp. Here, he explained, they must work. If they refused to work, they would go straight to the furnace. "Work or crematorium—the choice is yours," he said.

> **"Work or crematorium— the choice is yours."**
>
> – SS OFFICER

That night in the barracks, Elie found it impossible to sleep. The next morning, he and his father were moved again. As Elie marched through the iron gate of yet another camp, he read the sign above. ARBEIT MACHT FREI. Work makes you free. It wouldn't take Elie long to see the lie in that slogan. In this camp, the only freedom was death.

The next day, SS officers made the prisoners line up in front of a table cluttered with medical instruments. When Elie got to the front of the line he was told to roll up his sleeve. The man tattooed A-7713 on Elie's left arm. "From then on, I had no other name," Elie later said.

Less Than Human

The reason the Nazis were able to do such horrible things to other people was because they did not see the Jews as human beings. When the SS officers took away Elie's name and replaced it with a number, he ceased to be human. Elie later wrote about the experience: "Stripped of possessions, all human ties severed, the prisoners found themselves in a social and cultural void. 'Forget,' they were told, 'Forget where you came from; forget who you were.' Children looked like old men, old men whimpered like children. Men and women from every corner of Europe were suddenly reduced to nameless and faceless creatures desperate for the same ration of bread or soup, dreading the same end."

THE LABOR CAMP

After a few weeks in Auschwitz, Elie and his father were transported to Buna, a labor camp. At 4:30 in the morning, a bell sounded, ushering in a day of grueling labor and torture. After a cup of watery coffee, the labor units, or *Kommandos,* headed out to their jobs. Starving and frail prisoners were forced to carry brick blocks and push wheelbarrows at a run for 12 hours a day. If anyone attempted to rest, he was shot or beaten. When the prisoners returned to the barracks at the end of the day, they had to carry the bodies of those who had died at work.

Before the evening meal, the labor units had to line up for roll call. Although this task could have been done in 10 minutes, the SS officers dragged it out for hours to torture the prisoners. Prisoners had to squat or kneel with their hands raised up in the air the entire time. Anyone who fell or dropped his arms was shot immediately or clobbered. At the evening meal, Elie got a chunk of bread and some lard or margarine. Those who had missed the noon meal also got a bowl of cold, leftover cabbage or turnip soup. It was just enough food to survive—barely.

Day after day, Elie and his father walked through the same routine. Without nourishment, their bodies slowly shriveled, their skin exposing the bones beneath. Their only goal was to avoid the transports. If they became too weak, they would be sent to the gas chambers.

Elie often thought about his mother and sisters, especially little Tzipora. Deep down, Elie knew she was too young for work. Anyone who could not work was exterminated. Elie's father tried to comfort him. "Mother is still a young woman," Shlomo said. "She must be in a labor camp." Then, he added, "And Tzipora, she is a big girl now. She too must be in a camp." For the sake of each other and their sanity, Shlomo and Elie pretended it was true.

From time to time, Elie and the other prisoners had to go through a selection. The infamous Dr. Josef Mengele sat at a table as the prisoners filed past him. Mengele would write down the number of anyone he felt was too skinny, sick, or weak to work. Those prisoners would be sent to Birkenau—the extermination camp. Before one selection, the supervisor of Elie's barrack instructed the prisoners to move around, give themselves some color—and run. When Elie's turn came, he started running and did not stop until he had made it through the line. Afterward, he asked one of the others if the doctor had written his number down. "They couldn't have," the boy said, smiling. "You were running too fast."

Death Doctor

Dr. Josef Mengele, a German physician, was stationed at Auschwitz from May 1943 until January 20, 1945. Like the other Nazis, Dr. Mengele did not see prisoners such as Elie as human beings. They were just creatures in his eyes. Mengele was famous—and feared—among the prisoners for his horrific cruelty. Even other officers were afraid of him. Many Nazi doctors hated having to take part in selection. According to witnesses at Auschwitz, Mengele loved it. He had no problem killing. On one occasion he ordered the deaths of 1,000 people—

simply to stop an outbreak of typhus. He also liked to conduct painful experiments on the prisoners. Mengele was never captured after the war or punished for his brutal crimes. He drowned at a Brazilian resort in 1979.

WHERE IS GOD?

Some days when Elie and the others returned from work, they were forced to witness a hanging. The officers considered this a lesson. It was intended to keep the prisoners from acting out. Most of the time, Elie watched the executions with little emotion. Death was a common face in the camp. It rarely moved him anymore. There was one exception, though.

The supervisor of a particular Kommando was a Dutchman who had about 700 prisoners under his command. They all loved him like a brother. One of his aides was a beautiful young boy. The Gestapo discovered the Dutchman was working to sabotage the camp. They arrested him and condemned his young aide and two others to death.

As Elie lined up to watch the terrible sentence carried out, he noticed the three prisoners in chains. Standing on a chair in the shadows of the gallows was the little boy, a sad-eyed angel, as Elie called him. As the nooses were wrapped around the prisoners' necks, someone behind Elie asked, "Where is merciful God, where is He?" At the signal, the SS officers tipped over the three chairs. The entire camp fell silent.

> **"Where is merciful God, where is He?"**
>
> – PRISONER

The prisoners were forced to march past the victims and look at their faces. Everyone was weeping. The two men were no longer alive, but the third rope was still moving. The child, too light to break his neck in the fall, was still breathing. For more than half an hour, the officers made the prisoners stand in front of the struggling boy as he lingered between life and death. Behind

The World Was Silent

At Auschwitz, Elie asked his father how, in a civilized world, this kind of killing could be happening. Elie's father said, "The world must not know." Though it is true that most of the world did not know about these death camps, some people did. In early April of 1944—before Elie arrived in Auschwitz—aerial photographs of the camp had been snapped by Allied aircraft. These photos showed evidence of mass murder—the gas chambers and crematoria—as well as barracks for prisoners. A train, the railway ramp, and people being driven toward the gas chambers can also be seen in the pictures.

The photographs proved that leaders of the Allied forces— the United States, Great Britain, and Russia—knew about the concentration camps almost a year before the prisoners were liberated. After the war, Elie found out about these photographs. Even though he respected the Allied leaders, he was angrier at them than he was at his tormentors. The Allies knew what was happening, and yet they kept silent.

Elie, the same man asked again, "For God's sake, where is God?" Staring at the sad-eyed angel, Elie replied, "Where He is? This is where—hanging here from this gallows." ❖

When liberators arrived at Auschwitz, they found the
bodies of prisoners who died during the evacuation
lying in the snow outside the main gate.

CHAPTER FIVE

EVACUATION

I N DECEMBER 1944, ELIE GOT FROSTBITE ON HIS
foot. This was a common complaint among the prisoners.
Long hours in the freezing temperatures without proper
clothing and shoes ate away at their flesh. Elie was recuperating
in the infirmary in early January of 1945, when he heard the
rumors drifting through camp. From time to time, prisoners
overheard scraps of news from the outside world. They heard
that the Red Army was near, just a few miles or kilometers from
Auschwitz. The Russians had already liberated Warsaw, Poland.
Surely, they would be coming to Auschwitz next. As a precaution,
the Germans decided to evacuate all the prisoners. They would
relocate them to camps deeper in Nazi-occupied Poland.

Doctors told the patients in the infirmary that they would
be allowed to stay behind, but the patient in the bed next to
Elie was suspicious. He told Elie that Hitler had promised to

annihilate all the Jews. Certainly, the SS would kill the sick and injured on the spot, he reasoned. The Germans would leave no witnesses for the Russians to find. At first, Elie refused to believe this idea. Why should he care about what Hitler had said? The man stared at Elie with cold and tired eyes. "I have more faith in Hitler than in anyone else," he said. "He alone has kept his promises, all his promises, to the Jewish people."

> **"I have more faith in Hitler than in anyone else. He alone has kept his promises, all his promises, to the Jewish people."**
>
> – PRISONER

Elie was not afraid to die, but he was afraid of leaving his father alone. Elie knew that if he died, his father would have nothing left to live for. Elie ran out of the infirmary and asked his father what they should do. For once, they had a choice. Elie's doctor had said that if Shlomo pretended to be sick, he would be allowed to stay with Elie in the infirmary. Shlomo was worried that Elie would not be able to walk very far on his injured foot. But Elie worried that they would be killed if they stayed. At last, they decided to go. "Let's hope we won't regret it, Eliezer," said Shlomo.

On the morning of January 18, the bell rang at 6:00. What would turn out to be a funeral march began. The icy wind blew in violent gusts. Elie was freezing, yet he kept marching, carefully placing one foot in front of the other on the snow-covered ground. Anyone who could not keep up was shot. Elie kept telling himself: Keep running. Don't stop. All around him men collapsed in the snow.

The road seemed to go on forever. There was no stopping to rest, only the endless running. Elie wanted to collapse. "Death enveloped me, it suffocated me. It stuck to me like glue. I felt I could touch it," Elie remembered. Elie was chilled to the bone, starving, and his throat was parched. Still, he pushed ahead.

By the following morning, the prisoners had covered 12.5 miles (20 kilometers). Elie could no longer feel his legs, yet he kept moving like a robot. At last, the SS soldiers ordered the prisoners to halt. After a short break, the prisoners were ordered to march once more to a camp called Gleiwitz. At dawn on the third day, the SS divided the prisoners into two groups.

As Allied forces drew nearer to Auschwitz, the Nazis evacuated the camps. Prisoners were forced to march many miles to new camps. They were not given food or water during the long trek.

Those too weak to walk were moved to the left. Those who could still travel were ordered to the right. When Shlomo's turn came, an SS officer pointed to the left. Elie ran after his father as the officer shouted at him to come back. SS officers pushed their way through the crowd after Elie, but they couldn't catch him. He disappeared in the mass of men, who by this time all looked alike—pale, thin, and lifeless. In the confusion, some of the prisoners on the left shuffled to the right. Elie and his father were among them. For now, father and son would stay together.

The SS led the prisoners out of the camp to railroad tracks about a half-hour's march from Gleiwitz. A light snow continued to fall, forming little drifts on the prisoners' shoulders. One man began eating the snow off the back of another. Before long, the rest of the men had followed his lead. The afternoon ticked slowly by—minute by minute.

Late that evening, a train finally slowed to a stop in front of the men. It was made up of a long line of cattle cars. When Elie took his first train ride from Sighet in a car like this, 80 people fit inside. Now, the prisoners were so skinny that 100 could fit inside each wagon. The journey seemed to last forever. At last, they arrived at their final destination—Buchenwald.

A SON'S PAIN

When they arrived at Buchenwald, Elie noticed for the first time how much the death march had aged his father. Shlomo was sick with dysentery, a stomach illness that causes severe diarrhea. Every day, he grew weaker. His lips looked pale and thin. His skin had turned a grayish-brown color. One day, Shlomo started

After leaving Sighet, Elie and his family traveled to Auschwitz by train. He and his father were later marched to Gleiwitz, where they boarded a train for Buchenwald.

rambling. Certain he was dying, he told Elie where he had buried the family gold and silver. Elie pleaded with his father to hold on. Shlomo would not listen. "I tried to tell him that it was not over yet, that we would be going home together," Elie recalled, "but he no longer wanted to listen to me."

Shlomo grew worse by the day. Still, Elie refused to give up hope. He shared his bread and soup with his father and tried to comfort him. Although the block supervisor did not try to stop him, he offered Elie some advice. He said:

Listen to me, kid. Don't forget that you are in a concentration camp. In this place, it is every man for himself, and you cannot think of others. Not even your father. In this place, there is no such thing as a father, brother, friend. Each of us lives and dies alone. … Stop giving your ration of bread and soup to your old father. You cannot help him anymore.

On January 28, 1945, Elie pretended to be sick so he wouldn't have to go outside for roll call. He wanted to stay near his father. An SS officer passed between the bunks just as Shlomo called out, "My son, water. I'm burning up." The officer shouted at him to be quiet, but Shlomo was too delirious with fever to listen. "Eliezer," he called, "water." The officer came closer, still yelling at Shlomo to be quiet, but Shlomo continued to call out to his son. Finally, the officer struck Shlomo on the head with his club. In the bunk above, Elie laid still and silent, afraid to move. He knew that if he called attention to himself, he would be next in line for a beating—or worse. When Shlomo groaned and called out to his son again, the SS officer flew into a rage. "Be quiet, old man!" he screamed as he beat Shlomo viciously. "Eliezer! Eliezer!" Shlomo moaned once more. "Come, don't leave me alone." Elie later recalled how he felt at that moment:

Instead of sacrificing my miserable life and rushing to his side, taking his hand, reassuring him, showing him that he was not abandoned, that I was near him, that I felt his sorrow, instead of all that, I remained flat on my back, asking God to make my father stop calling my name, to make him stop crying. So afraid was I to incur the wrath of the SS.

After the guard left, Elie climbed down from his bunk and hovered over his father. Shlomo's lips were trembling. He was murmuring something. Elie stayed there for more than an hour. Then, he had to go to sleep. Elie awoke at dawn on January 29, and leaned over to look at his father's cot. Shlomo was gone.

Elie lived to see Buchenwald liberated. Here he looks out from his spot in the second row of bunks from the bottom, just to the left of the third post.

Another sick person had taken his place. The officers must have taken Shlomo away before daybreak, while Elie was still asleep. His father was dead, but 16-year-old Elie did not weep. Even though his heart was broken, he had no more tears.

"[My father's] last word had been my name," Elie remembered years later. "A summons. And I had not responded." When his father died, guilt took a stranglehold of Elie's heart. "I shall never forgive myself," he said.

After he lost his father, Elie sank into depression. Nothing mattered to him anymore. Three months passed as Elie went mechanically through his routine. By the beginning of April, American soldiers were close by. Finally, on April 11, 1945, Buchenwald was liberated—first by the resistance movement, and then by American soldiers.

Elie didn't know it until just a few days earlier, but there was a resistance movement inside the camp. They had smuggled in weapons and were waiting for the right time to unleash a revolt. On April 11, members of the resistance ran from barracks to barracks lobbing grenades. Elie and the other children lay flat on the floor as gunshots rang through the air and explosions shook the walls.

> **"[My father's] last word had been my name. And I had not responded. I shall never forgive myself."**
>
> – ELIE WIESEL

The battle didn't last long. At about 12:00, after just several hours of fighting, the SS fled and the resistance took over the camp. Six hours later, the first American tank rumbled up to the gates of Buchenwald.

Allied soldiers were eager to share their rations with the starving prisoners. Unfortunately, the food made many, including Elie, very sick.

LIBERATION

The American soldiers were shocked and horrified by what they saw in the camp. Prisoners who looked like walking skeletons wandered among heaps of dead bodies. For most of the soldiers, the sight was too much to handle. Seeing that the prisoners were starving, the soldiers immediately offered them whatever rations they had. Elie's first reaction was to stuff himself. Because he had not eaten in so long, the food was too rich for him. Just as he raised a piece of bacon to his lips, he fell unconscious.

Elie became seriously ill with stomach poisoning. He spent two weeks in the Buchenwald hospital, lingering between life and death. One day, he finally felt strong enough to get out of

After Buchenwald was liberated, hundreds of boys, including Elie, walked out of the children's barracks. It was their first taste of freedom in a very long time.

bed. He decided to look in a mirror and was shocked by the reflection staring back at him. Elie had not seen himself since he left home. He hardly recognized his own face. The person staring back at him looked like a corpse.

When Elie got out of the hospital, it took all his mental strength just to figure out where he was. He knew his father was dead. He was almost certain that his mother, his grandmother, and his little sister were dead, too. He hoped that Bea and Hilda might still be alive. Finding out would be the hard part. Lists of survivors soon began circulating. Elie did not see his sisters' names on any of them.

Elie couldn't wait to look for his sisters. He needed to decide where he was going to go. Some men from Sighet urged him to go home, but Elie, like many others,

was afraid to go back to his empty house. His whole family was gone. What did he have to go home to?

Then, word finally came. The children of Buchenwald, 400 of them ranging in age from six to 18 years old, had been invited to an orphanage in France. Elie did not know the language and wondered how difficult it would be to learn French. He actually had more pressing concerns, though. "First I had to learn—or relearn—to live," he later recalled. ❖

Elie (third row, fourth from left) and other children in his rescue group posed together in France in 1945.

CHAPTER SIX

LEARNING TO LIVE

GERMANY SURRENDERED ON MAY 7, 1945. THE war in Europe was over, but many Jewish survivors were afraid to return to their homes. Anti-Semitism still burned hot in many parts of Europe. Tens of thousands of homeless survivors migrated west to other European territories that had been liberated by the Allies.

In April, Elie took one more train ride. This time, though, there were no more cattle cars. He sat in a luxurious, second-class railroad car, especially reserved for the children of Buchenwald. Deep inside, however, Elie felt far from happy.

The trauma of the Holocaust did not end at liberation. Like other survivors, Elie was faced with the daunting task of learning to live again. He, too, tried to bury his nightmares and rediscover life. As he rode through the French countryside, Elie took a vow of silence. He decided never to speak of his experiences, until he found the right words. He doubted, though, that he would ever find the right words to describe the horrors he had witnessed. He didn't think people who hadn't been there could understand.

When Elie's train rolled into the depot, ladies from the children's rescue group *Oeuvre de Secour aux Enfants* (OSE) were there to greet it. Newspaper reporters and photographers also crowded the platform. Elie and the other children who had been rescued were big news. From there, the women took the bewildered children of Buchenwald to an orphanage. Like most of the others, Elie felt lost in a new country. Though he was one of many rescued children, Elie truly felt alone. In June 1945, he sat down in front of a blank page, picked up a pen, and started a journal. He began, "After the war, by the grace of God, blessed be His name, here I am in France. Far away. Alone." Words were his only friends, his only comfort.

Looking for a Home

Many Holocaust survivors ended up in refugee camps and displaced person (DP) camps. These camps were little improvement over the concentration camps. The survivors were treated like lepers or criminals. Again, they had to go through a new kind of selection. This time they had to prove they were healthy enough—both physically and mentally—to reenter "normal" society. "The suffering of the survivors did not end with the war," Elie later wrote. "Society wanted no part of them, either during or after."

Elie (in profile, back center) joined other Jewish orphans for religious services at the OSE children's home.

In Auschwitz, Elie had almost lost his faith, but he rediscovered religion right away. No matter how much he felt abandoned by God, Elie continued to pray. For him, it was an escape from the cruel madness of the world. Even though he was angry at what had happened to him, to his family, to millions of Jews, Elie did not fall prey to hate. Instead, he plunged into a universe of ideas and words. He threw open the books he had shut before the war. This choice saved him. Elie believes that if he had chosen hate and revenge, the feelings would have destroyed him.

One day the director of the orphanage told Elie he had a message from his sister. Elie could hardly believe his ears. Could one of his sisters really be alive? He was supposed to meet her in

Paris the following day. That night, Elie couldn't sleep. The next day, he took a train to Paris. When he stepped off the train, Elie saw Hilda waiting for him. As he rushed into his sister's arms, Elie's brain registered the fact that Hilda was alone. Perhaps Bea had died at Auschwitz. His fears were quickly calmed. Bea, too, was alive, but she had returned to Sighet in search of Elie. Meanwhile, Hilda had seen his photo in a French paper and contacted the orphanage.

After such a miraculous reunion, it was difficult to part again. Hilda and her new husband were desperately poor, however. They could barely afford to feed themselves. Elie returned to the care of the orphanage.

LOOKING TO THE FUTURE

After a month at the orphanage, the Jewish children were divided into two groups. Elie's group was transferred to the Château d'Amloy, in Vaucelles. Another group was leaving for Palestine in the Middle East. As far as Elie was concerned, the children in this group were the lucky ones. He had signed up to go with them, but his application was denied.

The OSE had a number of châteaux throughout France. As he grew up, Elie stayed in several of these castles. He continued to study, hoping someday he would be permitted to go to the Middle East. When Elie was 17, he moved to a château in Versailles, a city about 40 miles (64 km) from Paris. While he was there, he met François Wahl, a graduate student of philosophy at the prestigious Sorbonne University in Paris. Elie told François that he too would one day like to study philosophy at the Sorbonne.

The Promised Land

Ever since he was a young boy, Elie dreamed of "the promised land." The idea of moving toward a better life is a feature of the Jewish religion. Zionism is a political movement that uses those teachings to support the return of Jews to a homeland in the Middle East.

Zionists believe Jews should live in Israel, the Jewish state. During World War II, a Zionist group helped rescue Jews from Nazi-occupied Europe and take them to Palestine, where the Jewish state of Israel would be established. (A United Nations resolution, passed on November 29, 1947, called for the creation of a Jewish state and an Arab state in then-British Palestine.) Elie wanted desperately to be a part of a Jewish community again. He was not among the children chosen to go to Israel, however.

The idea of moving to the promised land became more of a reality in 1948, when the Jewish state of Israel declared independence.

François agreed to tutor Elie. He helped him master the French language and study classic literature. As Elie neared 18 years old, he realized that he would soon be an adult and out on his own. A whole new challenge was just around the corner. He would have to learn how to support himself alone—away from others who shared his past.

With Francois's help, Elie was accepted at the Sorbonne University in 1947. He took courses in philosophy and psychology. Meanwhile, on November 29, 1947, the United Nations passed a resolution granting Jews the right to a sovereign homeland. Israel in Palestine had gained its independence. Now more than ever, Elie wanted to go there. Because he was not a citizen of any country, though, Elie could not get a certificate to go.

Elie attended the Sorbonne University in Paris. Today, the Sorbonne is still one of the world's most respected universities.

He found a way around the problem in 1949. Elie took a job as a foreign correspondent for a French newspaper. He would travel to Israel to report on the new nation and immigration.

In Israel, Elie walked the streets of Jerusalem for the first time—though it felt as if he had been there before. Elie heard many Holocaust survivors talking about what had happened to them. Unlike other refugees, who spoke of nothing else, Elie never mentioned his experiences.

After four months in Israel, Elie took another job, this time for an Israeli newspaper. He would work as a Paris correspondent. For seven years, Elie traveled all over Europe. Each trip offered a new discovery. Elie's most important discovery—about himself—was yet to be made, however.

An Unfriendly Welcome

In Israel, the new immigrants had some surprising stories. They explained to Elie that the Israelis would not accept them. The survivors of the concentration camps were treated like outcasts. Many of the Israeli Jews felt the Holocaust survivors should blame themselves for their suffering. They believed the people should have left Europe earlier or risen up against the Germans. Proud Israelis commented, "Six million of you let yourselves be led like lambs to the slaughter." They looked down on the new immigrants, whom many of them saw as cowards.

A NEW BEGINNING

In 1954, Elie was sent to interview the French writer François Mauriac. Usually, when foreign journalists visited Mauriac, he was cautious. He was always afraid he would say something they might use to write unfavorable things about France. Mauriac knew immediately that Elie was different, however. He felt like he was talking with an old friend.

The conversation between the men soon grew personal. Mauriac began sharing with Elie his memories of when the Germans occupied France during World War II. He confided

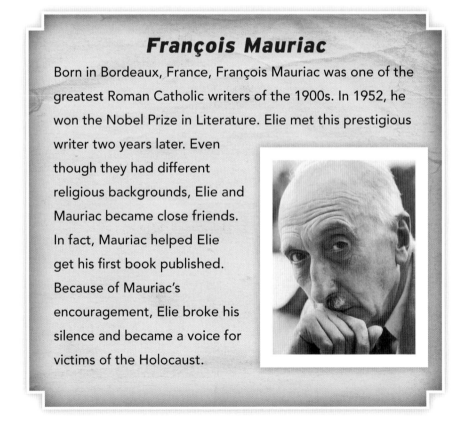

François Mauriac

Born in Bordeaux, France, François Mauriac was one of the greatest Roman Catholic writers of the 1900s. In 1952, he won the Nobel Prize in Literature. Elie met this prestigious writer two years later. Even though they had different religious backgrounds, Elie and Mauriac became close friends. In fact, Mauriac helped Elie get his first book published. Because of Mauriac's encouragement, Elie broke his silence and became a voice for victims of the Holocaust.

that what affected him most about those days was the image of cattle cars filled with Jewish children at the Austerlitz train station. Mauriac had not seen them with his own eyes—his wife described the scene to him. Still, the picture was engraved in his mind as though he had witnessed it himself.

Mauriac said he was outraged that these poor little children had been torn away from their mothers. At that time, he did not know about Nazi extermination methods. He could not even imagine something so horrible. His only thought when he heard about the children was of families being ripped apart. "I have thought of these children so many times!" Mauriac told Elie with a sigh. "I was one of them," Elie responded.

Elie told Mauriac about all the suffering he had seen during the Holocaust. He recalled the thousands of children who died. "And we do not talk about it," Elie said. Suddenly, Mauriac began to silently sob.

Elie felt uncomfortable; he had made Mauriac cry. He quickly got up and left the office. As Elie waited for the elevator, Mauriac tapped him on the shoulder and asked him to come back.

The two men went back into the office and sat down in exactly the same places they had before. For a long time, neither one of them spoke. The silence made Elie feel heavy inside. At last, Mauriac broke the stillness. "Maybe you are wrong," he said very softly. "Maybe you should talk about it." As Elie left the meeting that day, he thought about Mauriac's words. For 10 years, he had remained silent. Now, he felt, it was finally time to speak. ❖

Elie has read almost every book about the Holocaust, hoping to better understand what happened. He knows there could never be a good explanation, however.

CHAPTER SEVEN

Breaking the Silence

E LIE, WHO THOUGHT OF HIMSELF AS WEAK, WAS never sure how he survived the Holocaust. Perhaps now he knew why. Perhaps it was his duty to bear witness to the horrors he had seen.

When the war first ended, Elie knew that he had many things to say. Yet he didn't have the words to say them. Only those who were there truly knew what Auschwitz was like. Others, he believed, would never know. As time went on, though, he started to wonder if they at least could understand. Elie realized that he had to break the silence. He had to try to put the unspeakable into words.

In 1955, Elie began writing about his experiences in Auschwitz. He titled the nearly 900-page story, written in Yiddish, *And the World Remained Silent*. Elie chose that title for the book for a reason. Even though many people knew what was happening, no one stood up for the Jews before or during the Holocaust. No one spoke out against their persecution. Elie rewrote a shortened version of the book titled *La Nuit,* which was published in 1957. In 1960, the memoir was translated into English as *Night.* In the book, Elie finally allows his memories to break free:

> *NEVER SHALL I FORGET that night, the first night in camp, that turned my life into one long night seven times sealed.*
> *Never shall I forget that smoke.*
> *Never shall I forget the small faces of the children whose bodies I saw transformed into smoke under the silent sky.*
> *Never shall I forget those flames that consumed my faith forever.*
> *Never shall I forget the nocturnal silence that deprived me for all eternity of the desire to live.*
> *Never shall I forget those moments that murdered my God and my soul and turned my dreams to ashes.*
> *Never shall I forget those things, even were I condemned to live as long as God himself.*
> *Never.*

"The witness has forced himself to testify," he wrote. "For the youth of today, for the children who will be born tomorrow. He does not want his past to become their future." Elie was not only writing for the sake of those who came after him, however. He also hoped to honor those who had made the ultimate sacrifice. "To forget the dead would be akin to killing them a second time," he said.

Night

Elie Wiesel's memoir *Night* is one of the most widely read Holocaust books for students. Each year, hundreds of thousands of students around the world are touched by Elie's gripping and heart-breaking account of how he survived a Nazi death camp as a teenager. *Night* has also been featured in Oprah's Book Club. On her web site, Oprah offers special links, discussion questions, and an excerpt of the book. "After I first read his memoir *Night* seven years ago," Oprah said in her magazine *O*, "I was not the same—you can't be the same after hearing how Elie, at age 15, survived the horror of the Holocaust death camps. Through his eyes, we witness the depths of both human cruelty and human grace—and we're left grappling with what remains of Elie, a teenage boy caught between the two. I gain courage from his courage."

COMING TO AMERICA

In 1956, Elie took another giant leap. His editor at the paper in Israel suggested Elie work as a correspondent in New York City. In America, Elie had to survive on a meager salary of $175 a month. Some days he couldn't even afford to eat. Then a colleague helped Elie secure a desk in the United Nations (U.N.) press room. The extra money was helpful, and Elie loved spending time at the center of world diplomacy.

Messenger of Peace

The United Nations (U.N.), located in New York City, is made up of representatives of 192 countries. In addition to peacekeeping and humanitarian assistance, the U.N. works to promote respect for human rights, protect the environment, fight disease, and reduce poverty around the world. The United Nations Messengers of Peace are distinguished individuals, carefully selected from the fields of art, literature, music, and sports, who have agreed to help focus worldwide attention on the work of the U.N. These messengers volunteer their time, talent, and passion for humanity to raise awareness of the U.N. and its efforts to improve the lives of people everywhere. Elie has served as a U.N. Messenger of Peace since 1998.

When Elie first came to New York as a journalist, he traveled on French identity papers. He had a visa that allowed him to work in the United States for one year. When his visa was about to expire, Elie went to the French Consulate in New York to have his papers renewed. He was told that the consul could not help him. In order for his papers to be extended, he would have to return to Paris.

In desperation, Elie went to the U.S. Immigration Service. "Why don't you become a U.S. resident?" one of the officers there asked him. "Then you can apply for American citizenship."

Elie was surprised—and delighted. It was the first time someone had ever offered him a home. Before this, for his entire adult life, he had been a man without a country. Elie became a citizen of the United States.

More and more, Elie found himself wanting to write. He devoted four hours a day—from 6:00 to 10:00 each morning—to words. After *Night,* he wrote a novel, *Dawn,* about a concentration camp survivor. While *Night* was a historical memoir of Elie's experiences, *Dawn* was a fictional novel. At the same time, *Dawn,* like all of Elie's novels, is based on his memories and

Since Elie broke his vow of silence, he has become a voice for millions of suffering and oppressed people throughout the world.

experiences. Then, in quick succession, he wrote *The Accident* (1961), *The Town Beyond the Wall* (1962), *The Gates of the Forest* (1964), and *Legends of Our Time* (1966). These were all novels about Jewish suffering during and after the Holocaust. Elie first wrote his books in French, and they were later translated into English.

The Novelist

Elie continues to write novels. Even though all of his works in some way reflect his experiences as a Holocaust survivor, he asserts that his main theme is not the Holocaust. In fact, Elie has written more books on other subjects than he has about the Holocaust. For example, *Dawn* is a novel examining human empathy, or the ability to feel for others. In the story, a young concentration-camp survivor, Elisha, has been assigned to kill a British officer. The killing is payback for the scheduled execution of a young Jewish terrorist, who had been sentenced by British forces in Israel. Elisha is seriously conflicted about his assignment. He had been brought up to believe that killing is a mortal sin. Now, however, he must kill as an act of patriotism. Elisha is terribly burdened by the murder he is about to commit. He knows that a part of him will die with his victim. Another novel, *A Beggar in Jerusalem*, raises the philosophical question of why people kill.

After the English translation of *The Town Beyond the Wall*, Elie received the first of many literary awards, which would continue throughout his life. In France, he was awarded the *Prix Rivarol*. In the United States, he received the National Jewish Book Award from the Jewish Book Council. These prizes helped push the name Elie Wiesel into public light. The young man with sad eyes rose as a prominent new writer in the United States.

GOING HOME

In the fall of 1964, Elie journeyed back to his childhood home in Sighet. It was his first time back since the Nazis forced him and his family to leave 20 years earlier. Everything was the way Elie

In August 2002, Elie's childhood home in Sighet was turned into the Elie Wiesel Memorial House. The museum features a collection of photos and personal items belonging to the Jewish families that lived in the area before deportation.

> **"All those I love have perished, my little sister, my parents, my teachers, my friends. They have all vanished into fiery clouds."**
>
> – ELIE WIESEL

remembered it. It was almost as if time had stood still, waiting for his return. There was one difference, though. There were no more Jews in Sighet.

That night, Elie went home and stood in his yard on the poorly lit street. He passed his grandmother's house on the way. The window where Grandma Nissel used to lean out to call to him after school was closed tight. As Elie pushed open the gate in front of his house, the hinges creaked just as they had when he was a child. Elie moved quietly, knowing a family inside was asleep, a family who would not recognize him. For a long moment, he stood staring at the dark house. Suddenly, panic seized him. He remembered frantically burying his grandfather's gold watch the night before his family left their home forever. Elie began clawing at the dirt. His fingernails broke and his fingers began to bleed, but Elie continued to dig. He was numb to the pain. At last his fingers touched a metal box.

Elie opened the box and found the watch still inside, covered in dirt and rust. His raised it to his lips and kissed it. Kneeling there in the dark, Elie remembered his family:

All those I love have perished, my little sister, my parents my teachers, my friends. They have all vanished into fiery clouds. Only this thing—this nameless, lifeless, thing—has survived to welcome me.

Elie was startled by the sound of a dog barking. At once, he felt like a thief, even though he had done nothing wrong. Elie put the watch back in the box and buried it again under the tree. He remembers what he thought that night:

One day a child will play in the garden. He will dig beneath the tree and find the watch. He will thus learn that his parents were usurpers. And that among the inhabitants of his town, once upon a time, there were Jews and Jewish children. And that these children's futures had been stripped from them.

Elie stayed only one night in Sighet. The sadness and loneliness he felt there were too powerful. Over the years, Elie made other trips to Sighet, but he never stayed more than a single night. He has visited the past in his mind, however. Too many times to count. ❖

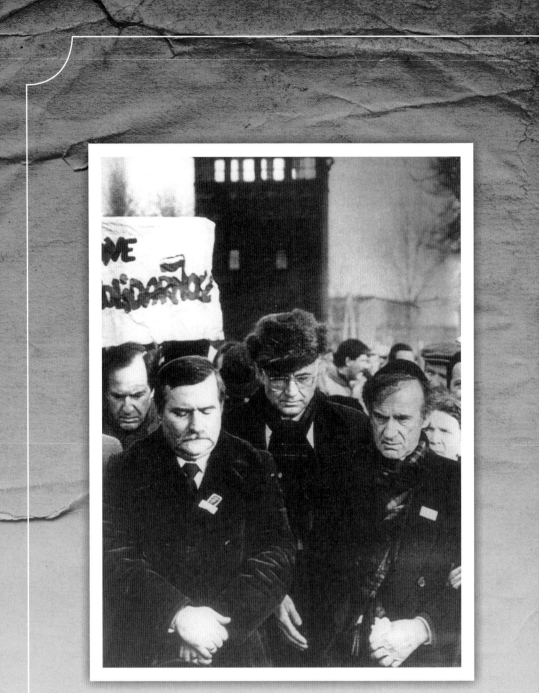

In January 1988, Elie (right) returned to Auschwitz with fellow Nobel laureate, Lech Walesa (left).

CHAPTER EIGHT

WITNESS FOR THE VOICELESS

AFTER ELIE RETURNED FROM SIGHET IN 1964, he traveled to Moscow and other Russian cities. For several years, rumors had been trickling out of Russia that Jews there were being persecuted. Because Russia's communist government had isolated itself from the rest of the world, there was no real way of knowing what was going on there or what kind of help the Soviet Jews needed. Elie wanted to see for himself what was really happening

On his first evening there, just a few hours after his arrival, Elie met a Soviet Jew. Elie was standing on the sidewalk outside of a synagogue. A man standing in the darkness asked Elie if he spoke Yiddish. When he said yes, the man knew Elie was also a Jew—but a Jew from another place. The man remained in the safety of the shadows, refusing to show his face. Elie could barely hear the man's voice. The few ragged sentences whispered in his ear were choked and afraid, but they were enough to describe the troubles facing Soviet Jews.

The man told Elie how Jewish life in Russia was very difficult. Teaching the Torah, the books of Jewish scriptures, was outlawed. Anti-Semitism was widespread. Worst of all, the Jewish spirit was deteriorating. "There is no time," the man whispered urgently. "You must understand. If I am being watched, I will pay for this conversation. Do not forget." Elie wanted to shake the man's hand, but he did not dare. Maybe someone really was watching them. He had only been in the country a few hours, but already Elie understood the fear and paranoia of being a Jew in Russia.

Even though it had been outlawed, Russian Jews still gathered together in secret to read and study Jewish texts.

The Night of Murdered Poets

On the night of August 12, 1952, Russian dictator Joseph Stalin secretly executed 13 Yiddish writers, poets, artists, musicians, and actors in the basement of Lubyanka Prison in Moscow. Ten Jewish engineers from the Stalin automobile factory were also killed that same night. The mass execution became known as the Night of Murdered Poets. The Russian government continued to suppress the Jewish religion and culture for decades. Jewish books and articles had to be smuggled into the country, and studying had to be done in secret.

When Elie returned to America, he wrote about what he had seen in Russia in *The Jews of Silence*. "I went to Russia drawn by the silence of its Jews," he wrote. "I brought back their cry." Elie's book drew attention to the Soviet Jews. Their struggles soon became the focus of humanitarian groups. These groups helped Jews emigrate from Russia to Israel and the United States.

Elie's experience with the Soviet Jews was a turning point in his life. Up until this time, he had served as a witness for those who had died in the Holocaust. With the Russian Jews, he was a witness for the living.

> "I went to Russia drawn by the silence of its Jews. I brought back their cry."
>
> – ELIE WIESEL

A WEDDING IN OLD JERUSALEM

In 1966, Elie was introduced to Marion Erster Rose. Elie was captivated by the way Marion talked about art, music, and the theater. A week after they were introduced, Elie invited Marion to lunch at an Italian restaurant. He ordered an omelette but never touched it. He just listened to Marion speak. Elie felt himself falling in love, but for the moment, he simply listened timidly. Before long they became friends, and eventually much more. Three years later, on April 2, 1969, the couple married at an ancient synagogue in the Old City of Jerusalem.

Elie and his wife have been married for more than four decades. In Marion, Elie found a true friend and companion for life.

A Wedding Blessing

According to Jewish custom, an orphan should go to meditate at the grave of his parents before his or her wedding day. Elie wanted to visit his parents the night before his wedding to invite them to the ceremony in spirit. Sadly, there was no grave to visit. Shlomo's and Sarah's ashes were mixed among those of the millions of others killed in concentration camps. Elie would not get the chance to visit with his parents that night or any other.

Elie's sisters Bea and Hilda were at the wedding with their families, as well as a few cousins and many friends. Elie, now 40 years old, thought about the people who weren't there—his mother, his father, Tzipora, and so many others. "The groom's mind wandered, seeking others who were absent," Elie later wrote. "For this was a day he had in some ways dreaded, and now he feared being unable to contain his emotions."

> **"The groom's mind wandered, seeking others who were absent. ... he feared being unable to contain his emotions."**
>
> – ELIE WIESEL

For a long time, Elie was opposed to having children. In his view, it was the ultimate expression of Jewish faith to have a child. The birth of a child is a declaration of hope for the future. Elie believed that the cruel and indifferent world did not deserve children. His wife convinced him otherwise. She told Elie that it would be wrong to give the killers one more victory. She argued that he must not let his long family line, and the Wiesel name, end with him. On June 6, 1972, Shlomo Elisha was born. The baby was named after Elie's father. For Elie, it was a beginning like no other. "I was the only son. I cannot break the chain," he decided. "It is impossible that 3,500 years should end with me, so I took these 3,500 years and put them on the shoulders of this little child."

> "I was the only son. I cannot break the chain. It is impossible that 3,500 years should end with me."
>
> – ELIE WIESEL

Still, Elie worried about the future of the world. Would it be a good place for his son? "When he was born, I felt sorry for him," Elie once said. "Now I still feel sympathy, but naturally the urge is much stronger than before to try to do what we can to make it a little better. Because he is here, we try."

TEACHER OF MEMORY

In 1972, Elie began teaching a course on the Holocaust at New York's City College. Many of his first students were children of survivors. He also continued writing. Six years later, Elie began a decades-long teaching career at Boston University as a professor in the Humanities, where he still teaches today.

For years, Elie's life had been devoted to bearing witness to what happened during the Holocaust. He did this through his writings and his teaching. In November 1978,

President Jimmy Carter asked him to assume another role to help keep the memory of Holocaust victims alive. President Carter wanted Elie to chair a commission in charge of creating a monument in memory of Holocaust victims. Elie told Carter that he did not like the idea of a monument. Jews have never believed in statues or buildings. Elie suggested a teaching project instead, a national Day of Remembrance. The president agreed. Before he left the meeting, Elie had one more request. He wanted permission to launch an investigative mission at various death camp sites. Again, President Carter gave his approval. For the next six years, Elie served on the President's Commission on the Holocaust.

On April 24, 1979, the first Day of Remembrance was observed at the Capitol Rotunda in Washington, D.C. Hundreds of guests, including the president and Congress, stood in silence as Elie addressed the crowd:

Thirty-five years ago almost to the day, a small Jewish boy and his family, and all the occupants of their town, were herded together and taken into exile. Thirty-five years ago, the little boy and his father stood facing the flames which were to devour most of the world they had known, and the little boy asked his father whether this was not a nightmare from which they would awaken. Certainly what they were seeing could not take place in the middle of the 20th century in a civilized society. 'If this were true, the world would not be silent,' Elie said to his father. To which his father replied, 'Perhaps the world does not know.' The world knew and kept silent.

Elie thanked America and the president for remembering and asking other nations to also remember. "No other country, and its government, besides Israel," he said, "has issued or heeded such a call." On the first Day of Remembrance, Elie admitted, "Memory may perhaps be our only answer." Six long taper candles were lit to symbolize the six million Jewish victims of the Holocaust. Then, Elie led the crowd in Kaddish, the Jewish prayer for the dead.

Many on the Holocaust Commission still wanted to erect some kind of physical memorial, where Americans from all races and religions could learn and remember. Elie agreed that a museum and study center might be an appropriate American memorial. The United States Holocaust Memorial Museum in Washington, D.C., opened to the public on April 26, 1993. On

The Mourners' Prayer

Kaddish is the prayer spoken by those mourning the death of a loved one. Jewish law requires that Kaddish be recited during the first 11 months following the death of a loved one and on each anniversary of the death, the *Yahrtzeit*. There is no reference, no word even, about death in the prayer. Rather, the theme of Kaddish is the greatness of God, who controls the entire universe and its most favored creature, each human being. In this prayer, Jews also pray for peace—peace between nations, peace between individuals, and peace of mind.

HOLOCAUST MEMORI

In 1993, Elie (right) helped President Clinton light the eternal flame at the dedication of the United States Holocaust Memorial Museum in Washington, D.C.

April 22, Elie spoke at the dedication. He talked about his vision for the project. He said:

> *When President Carter entrusted me with this project in 1978, I was asked about that vision, and I wrote then one sentence: For the dead and the living, we must bear witness. For not only are we responsible for the memories of the dead, we are also responsible for what we are doing with those memories.*

Elie believed the museum would bring people together. In this place, he hoped they would feel united in memory. Perhaps then, too, the living and the dead could be brought together. ❖

In 1980, Elie became the founding chairman of the
United States Holocaust Memorial Council.

CHAPTER NINE

FIGHTING INDIFFERENCE

FTER WRITING *THE JEWS OF SILENCE,* ELIE started to speak out against oppression, whenever and wherever it occurred. He had become a prominent figure in world politics. He wanted to use whatever influence he had with world leaders to help effect change. The fact that no one stood up for the Jews in Europe during the Holocaust continued to haunt him. He also remembered how his father had always helped those in need. Now Elie wanted to follow Shlomo's example. He wanted to use his influence to be a voice for those who could not speak for themselves.

Elie continued writing, but it was not for money, not to entertain, nor to please. It was to help others. He explains:

Whenever I see that there is an area in which my voice could be heard ... I raise that voice. When I needed people to speak for me, there were no such people.

Even if he cannot save them, Elie feels it is important to acknowledge people's suffering and let them know that someone cares. As he explains it:

I think the greatest source of infinite danger in the world, to the world, is indifference. I've always believed that the opposite of love is not hate, but indifference, the opposite of art is not ugliness, but indifference. ... The opposite of life is not death but indifference to life and death. Indifference is the enemy.

In 1980, Elie saw a chance to make a real difference. Between 1975 and 1979, 1.7 million Cambodians died, mostly by starvation. The United Nations tried to deliver food to the people, but military groups were refusing to distribute the supplies. In early February 1980, Elie helped organize a "March for Survival" to deliver food to starving Cambodians. Journalists kept asking Elie why he was there. "There are no Jews here," they said. "It's not a Jewish tragedy." Elie answered, "When I needed people to come, they didn't. That's why I'm here."

> **"When I needed people to come, they didn't. That's why I'm here."**
>
> – ELIE WIESEL

In 1984, Elie was awarded the Congressional Gold Medal. This is the highest civilian award bestowed by the U.S. Congress. The medal goes to an individual who performs an outstanding deed or act in service to the United States. President Ronald Reagan awarded Elie the Congressional Gold Medal in recognition of his outstanding achievements to world literature and human rights.

In 1986, Elie was awarded the Nobel Prize for Peace. His son joined him onstage when he accepted the prize from Egil Aarvik, chairman of the Nobel committee.

In 1986, Elie was awarded the Nobel Prize for Peace. In his acceptance speech, Elie explained how silence only encourages the tormentor. "That is why I swore never to be silent whenever and wherever human beings endure suffering and humiliation," he said. He explained that when human lives are in danger, people must intervene, no matter where they might live. "Whenever men and women are persecuted because of their race, religion, or political views, that place must—at that moment—become the center of the universe," he said.

Elie realizes that he is just one person. He cannot help everyone. "But I can help one person—maybe—and that's how it began," he says. According to Elie, what hurts the victim most

The Nobel Prize

Each year since 1901, the Nobel Prize has been awarded for achievements in physics, chemistry, physiology, medicine, literature, and creating peace. The man behind this innovative, international prize was Alfred Nobel. Born in 1833 in Stockholm, Sweden, Nobel invented dynamite in 1866. On November 27, 1895, he wrote his will. He set aside a fund that would be distributed annually in the form of prizes to those who made the greatest contributions to humanity.

is feeling that he or she has been abandoned—that nobody cares. He understands his limitations. He cannot give freedom, fill a person's pockets with money, or cure their diseases. "But I can give that person the feeling that he or she is not abandoned, not forgotten," he says. That's why when there is a tragedy in the world, Elie Wiesel is there. He explains:

> One person of integrity can make a difference, a
> difference of life and death. What all these victims need
> above all is to know that they are not alone; that we are
> not forgetting them, that when their voices are stifled we
> shall lend them ours.

In 1988, Elie Wiesel and his wife, Marion, established the Elie Wiesel Foundation for Humanity. The foundation's mission, rooted in the memory of the Holocaust, is to combat global indifference, intolerance, and injustice. Its youth-focused programs promote acceptance, understanding, and equality.

TO AUSCHWITZ ONCE MORE

On a cold day in January 2006, Elie returned to Auschwitz. He had been there several times over the years, often as part of the March of the Living. This international educational program brings Jewish teens from all over the world to Poland on Holocaust Memorial Day to march from Auschwitz to Birkenau. For this

In 2005, sixty years after the liberation of Auschwitz, Israeli Prime Minister Ariel Sharon (right) and Elie (left) led 18,000 people in a March of the Living.

trip, which he felt would be his last, Elie was accompanied by Oprah Winfrey. The visit coincided with Oprah's placement of *Night* on her book club list. Elie and Oprah started at the entrance, where as a teenager, Elie arrived in a cattle car. They walked on to the site of crematorium number three, where the bodies of his mother and little sister were probably burned.

Next, Elie led Oprah to one of the few barracks still standing. He told her that prisoners were packed two or more to a bunk on straw mattresses. Rats, lice, and other vermin were rampant. Deadly outbreaks of dysentery, typhus, tuberculosis, and malaria wiped out entire sections of the camp. Inmates wore thin cotton uniforms year round, even in the bitter, harsh winters. Given only meager rations of stale bread and meatless soup, many starved to death. The average life span was barely four months. Elie explained how it was hard for him to be back. "When I come here, I'm not really alone," he said. "I think of them all the time, but here even more so."

At one point, they stopped to look at a huge pile of shoes. Elie said to Oprah:

> *Look how sad these shoes are, they are crying. They seem to say, 'Look at me and cry.' How many Nobel Prize winners died at the age of one? Two? And whose shoes are here? One of them could have discovered the remedy for cancer, for AIDS ...*

"The death of one child makes no sense. The death of millions—what sense could it make?"

– ELIE WIESEL

Elie reflected on the past and how much it hurts him to revisit it. "The anger here is in me—hate is not," he said. "I write and I teach and therefore, I believe anger must be a catalyst [a channel for his work]."

Elie has read almost every book on the Holocaust. Each time, he thinks he might find some explanation for what happened. The more he reads, the less he understands. He says:

> *The death of one child makes no sense. The death of millions—what sense could it make? Except for here, now we know. Whenever people could try to conduct such experiments against another people, we must be there to shout and say, No, we remember.*

What I Know for Sure

In O magazine, there is a column called "What I Know for Sure." In an interview with Elie in November 2000, Oprah asked him what it is that he knows for sure. He answered:

"I have no doubt that evil can be fought. I have no doubt that indifference is no option. ... I have no doubt that we are here for a purpose. ... I have no doubt that the human being is human simply because he or she is human and we have no right to say that a poor person, because he or she is poor, is less valid to society than the person who is rich."

GENOCIDE EMERGENCY

Starting in early 2003, genocide ravaged the Darfur region of Sudan, a country in Africa. Sudanese soldiers, known as the Janjaweed, were fighting rebel groups in the western region of Darfur. In the beginning, the Sudanese government combated the rebel attacks with assaults against civilians from the same ethnic groups as the rebel forces. The targeted victims were mostly from the Fur, Zaghawa, and Masaalit ethnic groups.

Hundreds of thousands of civilians died from violence, disease, and starvation. More than 2.5 million were driven from their homes, their villages burned, and their property stolen. Thousands of villages were completely destroyed, forcing more than 230,000 people to flee to neighboring Chad. Most displaced people remained trapped inside Darfur. Large-scale government attacks against civilians began to decline in 2005, but millions remain at risk. Most of the displaced are not returning home for fear that their villages will be attacked again. Nearly 400,000 have died. Millions are homeless and on the brink of starvation. More than 100 people die every day. The United Nations calls the genocide in Sudan today's greatest humanitarian crisis.

> **"Silence helps the killer, never his victims."**
> – ELIE WIESEL

In 2004, the United States Holocaust Memorial Museum declared a Genocide Emergency for Darfur. During a speech given on July 14, 2004, at the Graduate Center of the City University of New York, Elie referred to Sudan as "today's world capital of human pain, suffering, and agony." He pointed out that as free

Elie is honorary chairman of the Museum of Jewish Heritage—A Living Memorial to the Holocaust—in New York.

citizens of the world, Americans must pay attention, feel out-raged, and be moved by compassion to intervene. "What pains and hurts me most," he said, "is … While we sit here and discuss how to behave morally, both individually and collectively, over there, in Darfur and elsewhere in Sudan, human beings kill and die." In April 2006, Elie spoke at a rally on the National Mall in Washington, D.C., urging the tens of thousands of people gathered there to help bring an end to the genocide. "Silence helps the killer, never his victims," he said.

In 2005, the Dalai Lama presented Elie with the Light of Truth Award. The award recognizes significant contributions to the fight for human rights and democratic freedoms for the people of Tibet.

Many other world figures have tried to push the United States to intervene on behalf of Darfur. In 2005, actor George Clooney and his father journeyed to Sudan to document the crisis. His film, *A Journey to Darfur,* was released in 2008. Clooney hopes that the documentary will raise public awareness and encourage people to support efforts to bring peace to Darfur.

BRINGING A MESSIANIC MOMENT

Some situations, such as the crisis in Darfur, can make Elie feel frustrated and helpless. Yet he pushes himself to carry on. Maybe he can help, or maybe he cannot. At least he can show the victims that they are not alone. He says:

> *To save the life of a single child, no effort is superfluous. To make a tired old man smile is to perform an essential task. To defeat injustice and misfortune, if only for one instant, for a single victim, is to invent a new reason to hope.*

Elie believes that everyone should work to bring a "Messianic moment" to others. A Messianic moment is a fragment of hope or crusading spirit. Elie described it as giving a person, especially a child, a different way of looking at the world. Anyone, he believes, can bring this light to another human being.

Some people might see Elie as a dreamer. How can one ever rid the world of hatred, violence, and murder? Elie's response is simple and determined. "We must not become resigned," he said. "The criminals never do."

Why did Elie survive? He has no answer for that question. It was not a miracle. Whether one lived or died at Auschwitz was often a matter of luck. "There were people surely worthier than I," he said. Through his life, he has placed tremendous meaning on his survival. Out of the ashes of Auschwitz rose a voice, a witness. Elie Wiesel has transformed his life into a testament for all who have suffered and all who continue to suffer. ❖

TIME LINE

1928 Eliezer Wiesel is born in Sighet, Transylvania (now Romania), on September 30.

1933 Adolf Hitler is appointed chancellor of Germany.

1939 Germany invades Poland in September, sparking World War II in Europe.

1940 Romania cedes northern Transylvania—including Sighet—to Hungary in August.

1942 Elie's teacher is taken away for execution by the Nazis, but manages to survive. He returns to Sighet to warn the others.

1944 Germany occupies Hungary in March; Elie and his family are deported to Auschwitz in May. Elie's mother, grandmother, and little sister are exterminated at Birkenau. Elie, his father, and two older sisters are sent to labor camps.

1945 SS units evacuate Auschwitz in January. Soviet troops liberate the camp on January 27; Elie's father dies of dysentery and starvation at Buchenwald on January 28. U.S. troops liberate Buchenwald on April 11. Elie is sent to an orphanage in France. Germany surrenders on May 7; the war in Europe is over.

1948   Israel gains its independence on May 14. Elie begins work as a newspaper journalist.

1960   *Night,* the English translation of Elie's book about his experiences in Auschwitz, is published.

1964   Elie returns to his childhood home in Sighet for the first time.

1965   Elie travels to the Soviet Union to investigate the persecution of the Jews; he documents his experiences in Russia in *The Jews of Silence.*

1969   On April 2, Elie marries Marion Erster Rose.

1972   Elie and Marion's son Shlomo Elisha is born on June 6. Elie begins a four-year position as Distinguished Professor of Judaic Studies at the City University of New York.

1975   Elie receives the Jewish Heritage Award from Haifa University and the Holocaust Memorial Award from the New York Society of Clinical Psychologists.

1976   Elie starts his teaching career as the Andrew W. Mellon Professor in the Humanities at Boston University.

1978   President Jimmy Carter appoints Elie as chairman of the President's Commission on the Holocaust.

1980   Elie is awarded the *Prix Liber Inter* from France, the S.Y. Agnon Medal, and the Jabotinsky Medal from the state of Israel.

1985   President Reagan presents Elie with the Congressional Gold Medal of Achievement.

1986   Elie wins the Nobel Prize for Peace in December; soon after, he and Marion establish the Elie Wiesel Foundation for Humanity, an organization to fight indifference, intolerance, and injustice.

1993   The United States Holocaust Memorial Museum is dedicated on April 22; Elie speaks at the ceremony.

2001   Elie speaks at the Day of Remembrance ceremony in the Capitol Rotunda in Washington, D.C.; he is granted the rank of *Grand-Croix* in the French Legion of Honor.

2005   Elie receives the Man of the Year Award from the Tel Aviv Museum of Art and the Light of Truth Award from the International Campaign for Tibet.

2006   At age 78, Elie takes what will probably be his last trip to Auschwitz. He goes there with Oprah Winfrey.

2008   Elie attends the World Economic Forum in Switzerland.

A CONVERSATION WITH
Sara Bloomfield

In 1986, Sara Bloomfield joined the United States Holocaust Memorial Museum (USHMM) in Washington, D.C., when it was in development. She served in several positions before becoming director in 1999. Here, Sara talks about Elie's influence and impact on the world.

Q: How do you think Elie's life and work have impacted the world?

A: Elie has devoted his life to giving a voice to those who have been silenced, especially victims of genocide. Elie believes evil will never disappear, but we must constantly fight the danger of indifference to evil. He has traveled the world wherever victims of genocide have suffered to ensure that in addition to other crimes, they will not also endure the crime of silence and indifference. He has inspired people worldwide to speak out when they see hatred and injustice.

Q: In what ways has Elie inspired your life and work?

A: I first read *Night* as a teenager and was deeply moved. Later when I was a teacher in Sydney, Australia, I taught *Night* to my seventh grade class. My students had never seen a Jewish person, and when they discovered I was a Jew, many of them displayed shock and others more overtly anti-Semitic attitudes. I tried to turn the experience into a learning opportunity, and I think it made a strong impression on all of us.

Q: What is the mission of the USHMM?

A: To serve as America's national institution for the documentation, study, and interpretation of Holocaust history and as a memorial to the millions of people murdered during the Holocaust. As a living memorial to the victims of the Holocaust, the museum strives to inspire leaders and citizens to confront hatred, prevent genocide, promote human dignity and strengthen democracy. As Elie wrote, "a memorial unresponsive to the future would violate the memory of the past."

Q: At Elie's suggestion, the first Day of Remembrance was held on April 24, 1979, in Washington, D.C. How do people continue to observe Days of Remembrance?

A: The museum sponsors our nation's commemoration in the rotunda of the United States Capitol every year. There is also an all-day reading of the names of victims in the museum's Hall of Remembrance. Other ceremonies take place at Holocaust centers, in state capitals, city halls, at synagogues, and churches and on military installations all across the U.S. and abroad.

Q: Why is it so important to remember the Holocaust?

A: The Holocaust was a watershed event in the 20th century, but its lessons are timeless. The Holocaust teaches fundamental truths about human nature, including the continuing problem of evil and mankind's tendency to see others who are different as "less than." The Holocaust also teaches that even the most advanced societies are not immune from collapse. Progress in technology, science, education, and government does not mean moral progress.

Q: What types of things can kids do to confront hatred and genocide?

A: Before action can be taken to prevent or stop hatred and genocide, people of all ages need to know what is happening in their communities and around the world. Kids should read the newspaper and follow the news. Technology can also play an important role. The Holocaust Museum is using Google Earth to track the genocide in Darfur. Armed with this knowledge, kids can inform others, including their parents, elected officials, and news organizations. Students in many schools have formed groups to educate others about Darfur. Churches, synagogues, mosques, and other groups around the country are also working to make a difference.

Q: What lessons can kids take from Elie's life?

A: Elie was born into a wonderful, close-knit, and loving family. Then during the Holocaust all of this was horribly taken away from him. He could have easily responded with hate, anger, and despair, and yet he did not. He resolved to rebuild his life and devote it to helping others—by speaking out, confronting injustice, and working to create a more peaceful world.

GLOSSARY

anti-Semitism: hatred of people of the Jewish religion

barracks: the buildings where soldiers and prisoners sleep

concentration camp: a camp where prisoners are detained, such as the places in Nazi-occupied Europe where Jews were tortured and murdered

crematorium: a building where bodies are burned to ashes

Day of Remembrance: the national day set aside to remember victims of the Holocaust

deportation: when someone is sent out of a place, such as when Jews were forced from their homes and taken to concentration camps

gas chambers: the rooms where concentration camp prisoners were killed with poison gas

genocide: the systematic killing of an entire race of people or nation

Gestapo: the secret Nazi police force

ghetto: an unusually poor section of a town, such as the sections of some European cities to which Jewish people were restricted in the 1940s

heder: a school for Jewish children

indifference: being unconcerned

Kaddish: the Jewish prayer for the dead

Kommando: a labor unit in the concentration camps

liberate: to set free

Nazi: the political party in Germany led by Adolf Hitler

patriarch: the father or head of a family or tribe

pogrom: an organized riot or massacre

ranks: rows or lines of prisoners

Red Army: the Russian army

resistance movement: a group that defies a governing body, such as the movement that fought the Nazis and helped concentration camp prisoners

selection: the process of inspection that each concentration camp prisoner had to go through, which decided whether he or she would live or die

SS: the core of the Nazi terror operation, which persecuted and tortured Jewish people

Talmud: the writings of Jewish law

Torah: the Hebrew Bible

transports: the string of cattle cars that carried the Jews to concentration camps

typhus: a disease that features high fevers, coughing, headaches, and other symptoms

witness: someone who gives testimony of a crime or injustice

Yiddish: an ancient Jewish language

Zionism: a political movement that supports the return of Jewish people to a homeland, a region now identified as the state of Israel

FOR MORE INFORMATION

BOOKS AND OTHER RESOURCES

Stern, Ellen Norman. *Elie Wiesel, Witness for Life*. Philadelphia: Jewish Publication Society, 1996.

Wiesel, Elie. *After the Darkness: Reflections on the Holocaust*. New York: Schocken Books, 2002.

Wiesel, Elie. *All Rivers Run to the Sea: Memoirs*. New York: Alfred A. Knopf, 1996.

Wiesel, Elie. *From the Kingdom of Memory: Reminiscences*. New York: Knopf Publishing Group, 1995.

Wiesel, Elie. *Night*. New York: Hill and Wang, 2006.

Elie Wiesel: First Person Singular. Alexandria, Virginia: PBS DVD, 2002.

WEB SITES

The Elie Wiesel Foundation for Humanity
www.eliewieselfoundation.org
Visit the official web site of the Elie Wiesel Foundation for Humanity to learn more about the organization.

The United States Holocaust Memorial Museum
www.ushmm.org
Discover more about the Holocaust, Day of Remembrance, and current genocide emergencies at the United States Holocaust Memorial Museum web site.

SELECT BIBLIOGRAPHY AND SOURCE NOTES

Greene, Joshua M., and Shiva Kumar. *Witness: Voices from the Holocaust.* N.Y.: Free Press, 2000.

Levi, Primo. *Survival in Auschwitz.* N.Y.: Simon and Schuster, 1995.

Stern, Ellen Norman. *Elie Wiesel, Witness for Life.* Philadelphia: Jewish Publication Society, 1996.

Wiesel, Elie. *All Rivers Run to the Sea.* N.Y.: Alfred A. Knopf, 1996.

Wiesel, Elie. *And the Sea is Never Full.* N.Y.: Alfred A. Knopf, 1999.

Wiesel, Elie. *The Jews of Silence.* N.Y.: Holt, Rinehart and Winston, 1966.

Wiesel, Elie. *Night.* N.Y.: Hill and Wang, 2006.

PAGE 2

Wiesel, Elie. *Night.* N.Y.: Hill and Wang, 2006, p. 118–119

CHAPTER ONE

Page 8, line 2: Wiesel. *Night,* p. 24
Page 8, line 11: Ibid., pp. 24–25
Page 9, line 4: Ibid., p. 28
Page 9, line 18: Ibid., p. 28
Page 9, line 27: *A Portrait of Elie Wiesel.* Alexandria, Va.: PBS DVD, 2002
Page 11, line 2: Wiesel. *Night,* p. 28
Page 12, line 1: Ibid.
Page 13, line 4: *A Portrait of Elie Wiesel*

CHAPTER TWO

Page 17, line 1: *A Portrait of Elie Wiesel*
Page 18, line 10: Wiesel, Elie. *All Rivers Run to the Sea.* N.Y.: Alfred A. Knopf, 1996, p. 15

Page 21, line 19: Ibid., p. 19

CHAPTER THREE

Page 24, line 9: Wiesel, Elie. *All Rivers Run to the Sea,* p. 7
Page 25, line 6: Ibid.
Page 25, line 24: Wiesel. *Night,* p. 10
Page 26, line 4: Ibid.
Page 27, line 9: Ibid., p. 12
Page 28, line 15: Ibid., p. 16
Page 30, line 6: Ibid., p. 17
Page 30, line 15: Ibid., p. 19

CHAPTER FOUR

Page 33, line 3: Wiesel. *Night,* p. 29
Page 33, line 10: Ibid., p. 30
Page 35, line 2: Ibid., pp. 31–32
Page 35, line 9: Ibid., pp. 33–34
Page 36, line 9: Ibid., p. 38
Page 37, line 3: Ibid., p. 42
Page 38, line 2: Ibid., p. 46
Page 38, line 16: Ibid., p. 72
Page 38, line 27: Ibid., p. 65
Page 39, sidebar: Wiesel, Elie. "Hope, Despair, Memory," Nobel Lecture, December 11, 1986
Page 40, line 18: Wiesel. *Night,* p. 46
Page 41, line 5: Ibid., p. 72
Page 42, line 18: Ibid., p. 64
Page 43, line 1: Ibid., p. 65

CHAPTER FIVE

Page 46, line 5: Wiesel. *Night,* p. 86
Page 46, line 20: Wiesel, Elie. "Hope, Despair, Memory," Nobel Lecture, December 11, 1986
Page 47, line 2: Wiesel. *Night,* p. 89
Page 49, line 3: Ibid., pp. 110–111
Page 50, line 3: Ibid., p. xii
Page 50, line 13: Ibid., p. xi
Page 50, line 21: Ibid., p. xii
Page 50, line 25: Wiesel. *All Rivers Run to the Sea,* p. 98

Page 52, line 5: Wiesel. *Night*, p. xviii
Page 55, line 12: Wiesel. *All Rivers Run to the Sea*, p. 98

CHAPTER SIX
Page 58, line 13: Wiesel. *All Rivers Run to the Sea*, p. 110
Page 58, sidebar: Ibid., p. 145
Page 63, sidebar: *A Portrait of Elie Wiesel*
Page 65, line 10: Wiesel. *Night*, p. xviii
Page 65, line 15: Ibid.
Page 65, line 23: Ibid.

CHAPTER SEVEN
Page 68, line 6: Wiesel. *Night*, p. 34
Page 68, line 21: Ibid., p. xv
Page 68, line 26: Ibid.
Page 69, sidebar: http://www.oprah.com/article/omagazine/oprahscut/omag_200011_elie
Page 70, line 9: Stern, Ellen Norman. *Elie Wiesel, Witness for Life.* Philadelphia: Jewish Publication Society, 1996, p. 140
Page 74, line 24: *Elie Wiesel Goes Home*
Page 75, line 5: Ibid.

CHAPTER EIGHT
Page 78, line 6: Wiesel, Elie. *The Jews of Silence*. N.Y.: Holt, Rinehart and Winston, 1966, p. 10
Page 79, line 2: Ibid.
Page 81, line 5: Wiesel. *All Rivers Run to the Sea*, p. 416
Page 82, line 6: Stern. *Elie Wiesel, Witness for Life*, p. 175
Page 82, line 15: Ibid.
Page 83, line 16: www.ushmm.org/research/library/faq/languages/en/06/01/ceremon/index.php?content=wiesel
Page 84, line 2: Ibid.
Page 85, line 3: Ibid.

CHAPTER NINE
Page 87, line 13: *Facing Hate*. N.Y.: Mystic Fire Video, 1991
Page 88, line 4: Ibid.
Page 88, line 16: "Oprah's Cut with Elie Wiesel," November 2000, www.oprah.com/omagazine/200011/omag_200011_elie.jhtml
Page 89, line 3: Wiesel. *Night*, pp. 118–119
Page 89, line 6: Ibid.
Page 89, line 11: *First Person Singular*
Page 90, line 3: Ibid.
Page 90, line 7: Wiesel. *Night*, p. 120
Page 92, line 19: *Inside Auschwitz: The End of Time* as quoted on www.oprah.com/obc_classic/featbook/night/holo/holo_trip_350_101.jhtml
Page 92, line 23: Ibid.
Page 93, line 2: Ibid.
Page 93, line 8: "Oprah's Cut with Elie Wiesel"
Page 93, sidebar: Ibid.
Page 94, line 27: Wiesel, Elie. "On the Atrocities in Sudan," speech delivered at City University of New York on July 14, 2004, as quoted on the United States Holocaust Memorial Museum web site www.ushmm.org/conscience/alert/darfur/wiesel.htm
Page 95, line 2: Ibid.
Page 95, line 8: www.ushmm.org/museum/focus/wiesel/
Page 97, line 6: Wiesel, Elie. *And the Sea is Never Full*. N.Y.: Alfred A. Knopf, 1999, p. 403
Page 97, line 18: Ibid., p. 396
Page 97, line 22: Ibid.

INDEX

ABOUT THE AUTHOR

Rachel Koestler-Grack has worked on nonfiction books as an editor and writer since 1999. She has worked extensively with historical topics—ranging from the Middle Ages to the Colonial Era to the civil rights movement. She has also written numerous biographies on a variety of historical and contemporary figures. Rachel lives with her husband and daughter in New Ulm, Minnesota.